SPAIN

A Land Blighted by Religion

BY JOSEPH LEWIS

AUTHOR OF THE TYRANNY OF GOD; LINCOLN, THE FREETHINKER; THE BIBLE UNMASKED; JEFFERSON, THE FREETHINKER; FRANKLIN, THE FREETHINKER; BURBANK, THE INFIDEL; VOLTAIRE, THE INCOMPARABLE; ATHEISM; THE BIBLE AND THE PUBLIC SCHOOLS; SHOULD CHILDREN RECEIVE RELIGIOUS INSTRUCTION?

NEW YORK
Freethought Press Association
1933

Copyright, 1933, by
Freethought Press Association, Inc.

AFFECTIONATELY DEDICATED
TO MY
WIFE, FAY
FOR HER HELPFUL COMPANIONSHIP
ON MY VISIT TO
THE LAND BLIGHTED BY RELIGION

CONTENTS

	PAGE
TEN DAYS FROM NEW YORK	9
CADIZ AND SEVILLE	13
CORDOVA	26
GRANADA	36
MALAGA	54
MADRID	57
ESCORIAL	71
VALLADOLID	75
TOLEDO	80
BARCELONA	86
THE NEW SPAIN	95

ILLUSTRATIONS

	PAGE
THE "AMBASSADORIAL HALL" IN THE ALCAZAR	15
THE TOWER OF THE GIRALDA	19
THE "DOLL'S COURT" IN THE ALCAZAR	21
CARDINAL MENDOZA	23
CORDOVA. THE OLD MOORISH MOSQUE CONVERTED INTO A CATHOLIC CATHEDRAL	27
CORDOVA. THE COURT OF COLUMNS IN THE MOSQUE	29
A GENERAL VIEW OF THE ALHAMBRA	37
A GARDEN IN THE GENERALIFE	41
THE COURT OF THE LIONS IN THE ALHAMBRA	43
THE HALL OF JUSTICE IN THE ALHAMBRA	51
MADRID. THE ENTRANCE MARCH OF THE BULL-FIGHTERS IN THE ARENA	63
THE PAINTING BY FRANCESCO RIZZI OF AN INQUISITION AUTO-DE-FÉ	67
THE ESCORIAL: ANCESTRAL HOME OF THE SPANISH KINGS	73
VALLADOLID. THE COURTYARD IN WHICH ARE STORED FLOATS FORMERLY USED IN RELIGIOUS PROCESSIONS	77
PANORAMIC VIEW OF TOLEDO	79
THE CATHEDRAL OF TOLEDO	81

ILLUSTRATIONS

	PAGE
SEVILLE. A COURT IN PILATE'S HOUSE	83
FRANCISCO FERRER AND FOUR COMPANIONS WHO WERE EXECUTED IN 1908 FOR THEIR OPPOSITION TO THE CATHOLIC CHURCH	89
THE ANCIENT BUILDINGS OF THE INQUISITION IN BARCELONA	93

TEN DAYS FROM NEW YORK

WHEN, in company with Mrs. Lewis, I boarded the S.S. *Rotterdam* on February 6th and sailed for the port of Cadiz, it was not the Spain that had been so cruel to my forbears that I cherished visiting, but a romantic Spain, a country of charm and beauty and song; of beautiful senoritas and brave and dashing caballeros; a Spain of magnificent castles and brilliant sunsets; of moonlit nights with reflection of the stars glittering like myriads of diamonds upon the matchless blue of the Mediterranean.

The dream was being fulfilled in all its anticipations.

The trip of ten days across the ocean was ideal. The waters of the sea were as calm as a lake and as blue as sapphires.

So smooth was the voyage, and so silently and swiftly did the ship plow through the water that the captain had to retard its speed to prevent our arriving before schedule time.

On a beautiful Sunday morning we arrived at the Island of Madeira. The reflection of the blue of the sky upon the placid waters gave it a hue the like of which I had never seen before.

From a distance, the narrow streets and unique build-

SPAIN: A LAND BLIGHTED BY RELIGION

ings on the island make it look something like a fairyland. However, this illusion is soon marred by the extreme poverty of the people, and the lack of sanitary conveniences.

Children barely out of their cradle pursue you with persistent begging. Begging, I found, was a profession taught early in childhood, and if one were to respond to all who approached for alms, one would soon have to join the already over-crowded army of beggars himself.

An ox-cart ride through the city revealed many interesting scenes. The streets are "paved" with small pebbles, with the sharp ends up, and the carts glide over the smooth-top surface like a sleigh over snow. Wheels on vehicles on the island are impractical, due to the steepness of the mountain sides.

A funicular took us to the top of the mountain, about thirty-five hundred feet above sea level. During the ride, which took about forty minutes, we were bombarded with flowers of all varieties thrown to us by boys and girls who lined the mountain side. If we kept the flowers we would throw them a coin; if not, we would return them. It seemed a pity to see so many beautiful flowers go to waste.

The funicular stops about one hundred feet below the top of the mountain. Here hammocks can be hired that are carried by two strong-bodied men from the landing of the funicular to the restaurant above, where we were to have lunch.

As is perfectly natural in a backward and priest-ridden country, the finest part of this mountain is dedicated to superstition, and devoted to the exploitation of the ignorant.

On the highest point and most valuable part of this mountain stands a fifty-foot cross, surmounted with a madonna and child, made of plaster of paris, on top of it. Oh, yes, the chapel is at the foot of the cross, so the poor deluded fools, after trudging their way to the top of the mountain, can conveniently part with their money.

For one who thinks of humanity first, the normal reaction after seeing this grotesque display of ignorance and superstition, is to think of the pitiful waste of such a beautiful site for so useless a purpose when it could be used to bring health to the sick.

The prevalence of consumption, in the Island of Madeira, I was told, is unusually high. This mountain top, swept by the pure air of the sea, and perfumed by the odors of sweet scented flowers should be, for the victims of this dreaded disease, a veritable paradise. However, they remain and suffer in their unventilated rooms while the cross withers under the curative rays of the sun.

Our descent was accomplished by the use of "baskets." These baskets provide seats for two or three, and are equipped with the same mechanism for sliding over the smooth top cobbles as are the ox-carts; with this exception. These baskets are guided by men, and a strenuous half-hour's work it is. Held back by ropes, so the gravitational pull will not dash us to pieces, we glide rapidly through the narrow streets of the village. Riding down in these baskets is like "shooting the chutes" at Coney Island.

SPAIN: A LAND BLIGHTED BY RELIGION

On the way from the village to the tender to take us back to our ship, we are accosted by numerous peddlers with all kinds of wares. These wares consist of everything from useless trinkets to "Madeira" wine that has just been imported from Portugal.

Just before the boat leaves, the merchants of the place come with their hand-made linen to make a final bargain with the tourists. They stand in their little boats, hold their wares high, and a spirited bargain follows.

CADIZ AND SEVILLE

WE hear the shrill blow of the whistle and the *Rotterdam* glides through the water for her next stop—Cadiz.

Cadiz is considered by some to be the most beautiful port in the world, and when Spain was in her glory, it was the most famous of its time. The sun is shining brightly, the *Rotterdam* is anchored again, in the distance we see Cadiz. The white houses glitter in the sunlight. Instantly one sees the beauty of the Moorish work.

Narrow streets to minimize the heat of the day; little balconies on the houses to provide a place to enjoy the cool of the evening.

A half hour visit through the streets, however, is all that is necessary to convince one of the lost glory and splendor of the place.

The Spanish Armada no longer proudly rides the seas. The two warships anchored at the docks are standing ready to take the enemies of the New Republic to places where they can no longer cause any trouble.

The customs officials at Cadiz evidently took us at our face value, for they gave us the courtesy of the port, and passed our baggage without investigation.

SPAIN: A LAND BLIGHTED BY RELIGION

That was the first of the many, many courtesies enjoyed by us during our travels through Spain.

An hour on a Spanish railroad is all that is needed to make one realize that it is not exactly like the trains of other countries. Perhaps the most important and strangest difference of all is that the wheels of the train are wider than on any other railroad in the world. This we are told was done so there could be no invasion of the country through this artery of transportation.

Within a half-hour's ride from Cadiz on the way to Seville, one is struck by peculiar cuts in the land that resemble small canals. Between these tiny canals are miniature pyramids of a white substance. Upon inquiry we find that this white substance is one of the most important essentials to life. It is salt! The ingenious cut in the land permits the waters of the ocean to flow in only to a certain height. It then evaporates by the heat of the sun, and a bed of salt remains. This is collected and built into these pyramids for storing and preservation. They cover miles of land.

Spain once supplied the world with salt, but this industry was not developed by the Spain of Isabella and Ferdinand. It was one of the rich legacies left by the former occupants and rulers of the country—the Moors. This is only one of the many rich legacies left in Spain by the Moors of which we will have much to say as we describe our journey.

Night is falling; we see in the distance a thousand shining electric lights. As the train approaches, I exclaim, "What is this?" And the answer is: "Seville."

THE "AMBASSADOR'S HALL" IN THE ALCAZAR.

SPAIN: A LAND BLIGHTED BY RELIGION

The mention of the name electrifies us. We gather our baggage quickly, put on our coats and wait for the train to pull into the station.

A night's rest, and then to see the fascinating city that has been made famous by song and story. I saw the shop where the composer of "The Barber of Seville" received his inspiration and wrote the lines of his now world famous opera. I saw the tobacco factory where worked the girl who has since been immortalized by the name of "Carmen."

I saw the cathedral, second in size only to St. Peter's in Rome, which was built upon the site formerly occupied by a Moorish mosque. This was built under the direction of the dean of the Cathedral who said that they would build a church so large that future generations would think them crazy. His prediction has come true.

The remains of Columbus are supposed to lie here.

Adjoining the cathedral is the famous Columbus library, founded by Columbus' son, Ferdinand. It contains the largest collection of material in the world concerning Columbus, and yet it lacks many of the most important items. One learns a great deal when one goes to Spain and discusses Columbus with the native Spaniards. They themselves wonder why there is so little actual information concerning the man who discovered America. They feel that many important facts concerning his life have been suppressed.

The belief that Columbus was of Jewish ancestry is prevalent throughout Spain. It would not be unusual,

CADIZ AND SEVILLE

considering the times in which he lived and especially the growing antagonism towards the Jews in Spain at the period, for him to have concealed his racial origin.

This fact is a thorn in the side of the Catholic Church. For years there has been a movement to canonize Columbus; but the pointed question is: How can they canonize a heretic who was a Jew!

In a glass case, as though it were still a silent witness, is a copy of a book, with marginal notations in Columbus' own hand, which formed the basis of his arguments to the Clergy, in justification of his belief in the rotundity of the earth.

This book is mute evidence that Columbus had been in prison and had been put "to the question" by the church; which means that he had been tortured in an effort to make him renounce his heresy. That he died in chains they do not deny. Their only explanation is that he was imprisoned for political reasons. Governments have been guilty of many unjust acts, and certainly the Spanish rulers are not without their long list of crimes, but it seems hardly probable that a man who had made so important a discovery as Columbus, and had so tremendously increased the wealth of the country should be repaid by so cruel an imprisonment. The efforts now of the Church to deny their part in the treatment of Columbus is only another instance which adds to their already disreputable reputation for hypocrisy and deceit.

I visited Huelva and the convent of La Rabida where Columbus spent the night before he set sail for the undiscovered shore.

SPAIN: A LAND BLIGHTED BY RELIGION

I saw the room in which he slept, and stood upon the spot now marked by a monument from which he boarded the *Santa Maria* that was to take him across the ocean.

Adjoining the cathedral of Seville is the world famous tower of the Cathedral—the Giralda.

I want to emphasize the fact that the Giralda was NOT built by the Spanish Catholics. And it was not built by the Moors as a part of the Mosque. When ignorant and brutal Catholicism found this tower they did not know what to do with it, so they made it part of the cathedral.

Perhaps many Spaniards themselves do not know the facts concerning this most unusual and beautiful piece of work. Originally, this tower had a glistening globe of gold on top of it. What would a Catholic country do with such a symbol that had just put into chains the man who had proved the earth a globe?

The Giralda, or Tower, of Seville was the first Astronomical tower built in Europe. It was erected under the superintendence of Gerber, the mathematician, in 1196. After the expulsion of the Moors, the Catholic rulers, not knowing what else to do with it, turned it into a belfry. They removed the globe and replaced it with a weather vane.

How the priests of this Catholic-ruled country perverted the uses of the arts and the sciences, we shall get a glimpse as we continue.

The first astronomical tower is not the only thing that the Moors brought to Spain and to Europe. And the discontinuance of its use and the destruction of its purpose

THE TOWER OF THE GIRALDA. THE ORNAMENTAL DESIGN PROVES THAT IT WAS BUILT BY THE MOORS FOR ASTRONOMICAL STUDIES.

is not the first and only thing that the Spain of Isabella and Ferdinand was responsible for. Their crimes reach an immeasurable enormity.

The Moors developed a scientific agriculture, which was regulated by a code of laws. To the cultivation of plants they devoted much attention. They introduced rice, sugar and cotton. They were past masters in building beautiful gardens and developing the orchard fruits. They brought the almond and the olive, the orange and the peach to Spain. Spain owes to the Moors the culture and manufacture of silk. They were experts in the breeding of cattle and especially the horse. It is said that the Moors had three loves. The horse was one of them. They bred the finest horses that man ever rode. The Andalusian horse was the prize animal of Europe.

They introduced the Egyptian system of irrigation by flood gates, wheels and pumps, and it is still called by the name they gave it.

They introduced the art of making pottery out of clay, and what is known today as "Dutch" tile is the invention of the Moors of Spain.

I saw the Alcazar, the palace of the Moorish kings. When one announces that he is going to Spain, and especially to Seville, he is told to be sure to see the Alcazar and the Giralda. We are not told, however, that these are not the works of Catholic Spain.

What a thing of beauty it is! With the exception of the Alhambra in Granada it stands as the most beautiful artistic building I have ever seen. Instantly, one recog-

THE "DOLL'S COURT" IN THE ALCAZAR.

nizes the inimitable Moorish work, with its touch of delicacy and beauty that remains unparalleled.

I wonder what thoughts must have passed through the minds of the Spanish kings when occupying this royal palace. I wonder if they ever considered themselves thieves, bandits and robbers. For that is what they were. They stole these palaces from the Moors.

I cannot describe this building; no picture can do it justice. It must be seen to be appreciated. I walked through Ambassadors Hall and sat upon the marble benches. Here, it is said, Columbus received from Isabella her final approval for his voyage across the ocean.

I walked through the rooms below, around the balcony above, and the more I saw the more my admiration increased for the builders that made this place.

The Moors never built a castle without a garden of equal beauty, and the one made for the Alcazar in Seville is no exception.

To my left from a corner of the balcony I saw something that did not belong there. It was a private chapel, built into one of the rooms for the exclusive use of Isabella. The crucifix was out of place in this building. This chapel was a mutilation and a desecration.

In the room adjoining the chapel was the bedroom of Isabella. It was also for the private use of her confessor, Mendoza. And what strange things religion does, loomed before me when I mentioned his name.

In the Columbus Library there is an oil painting of every father confessor of the Spanish rulers. They form a queer gallery of faces. When we came to the picture

CARDINAL MENDOZA, DESCENDENT OF JEWS, CONFESSOR
TO QUEEN ISABELLA, AND THREATENED BY THE
INQUISITION AS A "RELAPSED" CATHOLIC.

SPAIN: A LAND BLIGHTED BY RELIGION

of Mendoza there came to my mind this interesting story concerning him.

As Cardinal of Spain and as father confessor to the Queen, he was the most powerful man of the country. He was often referred to as the "third king." Mendoza was the grandchild of a *converso;* that is, a Jew who had accepted Christianity. He had only one rival, and an insolent one he was, too. This rival will never be forgotten either in the history of Spain or in the history of man. He should never be forgotten. He should always be remembered, so that such a man should never again live upon this earth. This man was Torquemada. He feared Mendoza because his influence over Isabella was becoming too great. He feared him; although Mendoza was true to every tenet of Catholicism. His rank as a Cardinal is a testimony to that.

After the establishment of the Inquisition Torquemada invoked the provisions of the second commandment against the Queen's confessor. Torquemada held the Bible supreme in authority in holding that the child must suffer for the sins of the father until the third and fourth generation. Only through the intercession of the Pope was Mendoza saved from being burnt at the stake.

And the strangest thing of all is that Torquemada himself had Jewish blood running through his veins.

Even Ferdinand, the consort of Isabella, was of Jewish descent.

Is it any wonder that such fanaticism brought to doom and destruction the glory that was once Spain?

One is touched to tears when one realizes the destruction brought to this once lovely city. Yes, the Moors and the Jews were driven out; that is, the artists and scientists were expelled, but even the stupid Catholic clergy hesitated to destroy the imperishable art that they had left.

Seville is still a city of charm and fascination. Four hundred years was still not enough to strip it completely of all of its former witchery.

The part of Seville formerly occupied by the Moors and the Jews still offers a residential area surpassed by no other city I have seen. They knew and practiced the art of making beautiful homes. They also knew the art of song, and joy and laughter. This also Catholicism was unable to suppress completely.

We visited the Kursal, watched the performances of Spanish dancers, and heard from their lips their Spanish songs, and I left Seville with the click of the castanets still ringing in my ears.

And the castanets too are a legacy left by the Moors.

CORDOVA

CORDOVA was our next stop.

If one was moved to tears at the destruction of the splendor that was Seville, then no emotion or words are adequate to describe the ruins of this magnificent city of the Moors—Cordova—by ruthless Christianity.

Here was built, in the eighth to tenth centuries, the famous Mezquita, acknowledged to be the most beautiful religious building in the world. One needs to see it but once to understand why it has been so universally praised. Yet not a single thing about this masterpiece of construction indicates that it was purposely designed for a house of worship. No cross, no image, no crescent; no symbol of any kind adorns it. Here the Moslem, the Christian, and the Jew; the Oriental and Occidental; the East and the West; could have met in perfect peace.

The Mezquita is one of those beautiful things man has made that is a joy forever. It measures 383 yards in length and 183 yards in width. It had 860 pillars of irreplaceable marble. Its ceilings were a work of art with a blending and harmony of colors that only the artisans that did the work could so beautifully execute. Its whole architecture is flawless. Its 37 arched open entrances per-

CORDOVA. THE OLD MOORISH MOSQUE CONVERTED INTO A CATHOLIC CATHEDRAL.

SPAIN: A LAND BLIGHTED BY RELIGION

mitted light to penetrate on all sides. Its numerous arches of red and white stone awe one into an inexpressible appreciation for the masters who built it. When the sword of Holy Catholicism captured this magnificent city, it reduced this intellectual center of Europe; this Mecca of scientists, artists and merchants; this thriving city of over 1,000,000 inhabitants, with their beautiful homes of balconies and terraces, of gardens and patios; to a miserable priest-contaminated serf community of 73,000! The destruction of Cordova was Christianity's "most unkindest cut of all."

After capturing this wonderful city, Catholicism cut the heart out of the Mezquita to erect within its walls a Christian church with all its hideous images and crude and repulsive trimmings. Beautiful arches have been closed to make chapels for the ignorant and superstitious. Where the Mezquita was a building of beauty and charm, of perfect symmetry and proportion, of blending of light and shadow, it is now but a symbol of the brutal destructiveness of Christianity.

Cordova was a city that any nation might have pointed to with pride. It has been said that a man might walk a straight line for ten miles by the light of the public lamps. The development and the state of progress of this city can best be realized when we consider that the city of London did not have a single street lamp until 700 years later! In Cordova the streets were solidly paved and kept in perfect condition, while in Paris at the same time no one could cross his threshold on a rainy day without stepping in mud up to his ankles. The beauti-

CORDOVA. THE COURT OF COLUMNS IN THE MOSQUE.

ful homes of Cordova, with their fountains of sparkling water and shady nooks for relief from the heat of the day, stand out in bold relief against the windowless and chimneyless houses of the rest of Europe.

Here and there in Cordova, one can still find homes with polished marble balconies, overhanging orange gardens, and courts with cascades of water.

The Moors had retiring rooms, vaulted with stained glass, speckled with gold, over which streams of water were made to gush; the floors and walls were of exquisite mosaic. One of the palaces had a fountain of quicksilver which shot up in a glistening spray, "The glittering particles falling with a tranquil sound like fairy bells." Another had apartments into which the cool air was drawn from the flower gardens in summer, by means of ventilating towers; in winter, through earthen pipes from vaults below, warm and perfumed air would permeate the rooms. Tapestry lined their walls, while the finest of Persian rugs covered their floors.

The Moors were a clean people. Not only did they have baths in their homes, but numerous public baths as well. But not one of the eight hundred and fifty public baths made from the marble taken from the Sierra Nevada Mountains remains today! They have all been destroyed and never replaced.

Of the three loves of the Moors, water was one of them. They were clean in body and in clothes. They taught Europe the use of the often changed and often washed undergarment that it still called by the name they gave it—the Chemise.

CORDOVA

The Catholic clergy taught their devotees many things that were next to God but cleanliness was not one of them. In fact, under Christianity at one time, the dirtier you were the more holy you were. Filth was synonymous with faith.

Draper is the authority for the statement that no Arab of any standing could clothe himself, in the custom of the European of his day, by wearing a garment until it dropped to pieces of itself; a loathsome mass of vermin, stench and rags.

It was impossible to find a representative Arab, contemporary with Thomas à Becket, who would have suffered such a spectacle as his corpse did when his haircloth shirt was removed. Simon Stylites, whose bodily odor was so repulsive that a person had to hold his nose when approaching him, was sainted by the Catholic Church!

Another great gulf separated the Moors of Spain from their Catholic neighbors.

The Moors were philosophers and scientists, their maxim being that the real learning of a man is of more public importance than any particular religious opinion he might entertain.

They had developed a fine literature; the Arabian Nights is still a world classic. Their institutions of learning were models of instruction; and their scientific discoveries of the very highest character. They introduced into Europe the Arabic numerals, the nine digits and the cipher, and as a result it caused a complete revolution in

SPAIN: A LAND BLIGHTED BY RELIGION

arithmetical computations. The word "cipher" in Arabic means a blank or void.

And while Catholic Christianity was asserting with all its absurdity the flatness of the earth, and punishing those who questioned its authority, the Spanish Moors—"those miserable infidels"—were teaching geography in their common schools from GLOBES.

Here Christopher Columbus came. It was here that he mingled with the scientific men of the time. It was here that he imbibed the scientific conception of the structure of the earth. No wonder he felt as certain of his discovery of finding a new land as that his key would open the door of his room.

In the library at Cairo, there is still preserved a globe of brass reputed to have belonged to the great astronomer Ptolemy. There is one that was made for Roger II of Sicily; and one that Gerber had brought from Cordova for use in the school he had established at Rheims!

The Arabs made many important astronomical discoveries, and gave the stars many of their names. They determined the length of the year, and were the first to use the pendulum oscillations as a measurement of time. They introduced the mariner's compass, knew the density of the air, and had made a table of specific gravities.

They introduced measurements by weight; the smallest being a grain of barley, four of which made one sweet pea, called in Arabic a *carat*. We still use this method originated by the Moors and we speak of gold being so many *carats* fine.

Here Averroes had promulgated the philosophy of the

Greeks. Here Maimonides was born, with the exception of Spinoza, the greatest thinker of the Jews. But perhaps more important than all was that the Moors had developed a philosophy of scepticism.

Here in 1058 Algazzali said: "My aim is simply to know the truth of things, consequently it is necessary for me to ascertan what is knowledge." And he gives this illustration: "Thus when I have ascertained ten to be more than three, if any one were to say, 'on the contrary, three is more than ten, and to prove the truth of my assertion, I will change this rod into a serpent,' and if he were to change it, my conviction of his error would remain unshaken. His maneuver would only produce in me admiration for his ability. I should not doubt my own knowledge."

And how well put is this, and with what understanding. "If we look at the stars, they seem to be as small as money pieces; but mathematical proofs convince us that they are larger than the earth. These and other things are judged by the senses, but rejected by reason as false. I abandoned the senses therefore, having seen all my confidence in their truth shaken."

Is it any wonder that the Catholic clergy looked with increasing hatred upon these people?

The progress of a people can be measured in direct proportion to the intensity of the philosophy of scepticism that they manifest.

Doubt, analysis and investigation are the three major principles of the philosophy of progress.

The Arabs had developed the science of Chemistry

to its highest point and had commenced the application of chemistry to the theory and practice of medicine. Syrup, julep, elixir and many other words are still used by apothecaries.

They enjoyed the reputation of being the foremost physicians of their age. And in Cordova, the physician Albucasis did not hesitate to perform the most difficult surgical operations. He left behind descriptions of the surgical instruments he employed. And we learn that in delicate operations on females the services of properly instructed women were secured.

What a contrast that was to the teachings of the Church! The Christian was taught that if he was feverstricken or met with an accident that he was being punished for some disobedience to God's will, and therefore rushed to the nearest shrine and prayed for a miracle. The Moors had better sense. They relied upon the prescription of their physician or the knife of the surgeon.

It shows the criminal destruction that Catholic Christianity brought to this country and its civilization.

Woe the day when Christianity destroyed the civilization of the Moors. No pen is capable of describing the loss to humanity that the spread of this intellectual Black Plague cost the human race.

Nothing remains today of the glory that was Cordova; this exquisite gem of the Moors, this city of almonds and oranges, of palms and olives, is but a shell of its former splendor. Christianity brought the sword and nothing more. Cordova has lain prostrate for nearly four centuries.

CORDOVA

We were in Cordova during the full moon, and I never saw the sky so blue, and I never saw the moon so brilliant, and I never saw night look so nearly like day as I did in Cordova.

What an appropriate place and time to celebrate one's eighteenth wedding anniversary!

GRANADA

AT six o'clock on a beautiful moon-lit morning we started in an automobile for Granada. The air was crisp, the sky clear as crystal, and the moon was still high in the heavens.

We began traveling with great speed over the country road. The gray hue of the moon-colored morning cast a silvery reflection through the olive and almond trees that covered the mountainsides.

It was not long however before the moon began to disappear below the horizon of the west, while the sun began to show its crimson ball over the horizon of the east.

I wonder how many have been so fortunate as to stand with outstretched hands to both the sun and the moon, bidding farewell to one and welcome to the other.

And just at this moment, directly in front of us stood the remains of a beautiful city of the Moors with a still more beautiful castle. It was Espejo, which in Moorish means "A Looking Glass." And I wonder where the Moors ever got such a beautiful name for such a beautiful place. I wonder if some one when building the Espejo gave it its name from the reflection cast by this

A GENERAL VIEW OF THE ALHAMBRA.

SPAIN: A LAND BLIGHTED BY RELIGION

unusual sun-moon morning that we had observed on our way to Granada.

We had little time to tarry along the roadside. We had taken an automobile to get to Granada in four hours instead of the train that required nine hours.

This meant that no time should be lost if we were to return to Cordova on scheduled time.

Although rapidly traveling with an automobile, I nevertheless could not help observe the vast uncultivated fields that lie between these two formerly great cities of Spain.

Miles upon miles of land remain untouched. The soil looks as if human hands have not touched it in centuries. This condition becomes so much more pronounced because here and there stands a primitive hut with a few souls working about it. I could not help remarking that in a country where there was so much poverty, why had this land, which could produce so much of the necessities of life, remained uncultivated. I pondered for a long time the reason for this condition, and no one seemed to be able to give us the proper answer. It was not until I came to Barcelona that I learned the real reason why this situation prevailed.

In Barcelona I found that during the past thousand years the wealthy of the community were forced, upon pain of excommunication, to leave their lands to the church. In return for this legacy the church would build a special chapel where the local priest would pray for the repose of the soul of the deceased. It did not take many generations for the land to become the property

GRANADA

of the church. And also it did not take many generations for these private chapels to become abandoned for priests of future generations would lose contact with the giver of the land for whom the chapel was built. His soul would have to rest content with the prayers of those who knew him. Since the church was not interested in the development of the land, deriving its revenue from other and less troublesome sources, these vast fields have remained uncultivated for centuries.

Down the valley and up the mountainsides we traveled, and just as we reached the summit of a rather high mountain, the chauffeur pointed out to us the Sierra Nevada mountains. There, directly in front of us, was one of the most inspiring scenes of the trip. Sierra Nevada we learn means "a range of snow-capped mountains." And how well these mountains were named. Nearer and nearer we come and soon we are to reach Granada.

Through the village and up a steep mountainside and we come to the famous Washington Irving Hotel.

Here we rested, and before a huge log fire we had our lunch, and what legends and reveries swiftly passed through our minds as we thought of Washington Irving and his stay in the Alhambra.

Next in importance to building a beautiful palace is the selection of a site that properly belongs to the building. How often have we seen beautiful buildings improperly placed, and beautiful sites with ugly and unbecoming buildings upon it. Nothing like that can be found here.

The Alhambra is built upon a mountain high above

Granada and gives one a complete panorama that must have been inspiring to those who occupied this palace and saw the seething life that once pulsated in the great city below.

Previously, I spoke of the destruction that the Spain of Isabella and Ferdinand brought to this beautiful country, and we would not have been privileged to see even this magnificent castle with its indescribably beautiful garden, were it not for the invasion of Spain by the French.

Perhaps the man who spent so much time in the Alhambra and who was really responsible for bringing its beauty to the attention of the world can best describe the reason for its preservation.

After telling of its abandonment by the Spanish rulers because of their superstition concerning earthquakes, and of its inhabitation by rogues and smugglers and the inevitable rapid destruction and decay, Washington Irving says:

"During the recent troubles in Spain, when Granada was in the hands of the French, the Alhambra was garrisoned by their troops, and the palace was occasionally inhabited by the French Commander. With that enlightened taste which has ever distinguished the French nation in their conquests, this monument of Moorish elegance and grandeur was rescued from the absolute ruin and desolation that was overwhelming it. The roofs were repaired, the salons and galleries protected from the weather, the gardens cultivated, the water courses restored, the fountains once more made to throw up

A GARDEN IN THE GENERALIFE.

sparkling showers; and Spain may thank her invaders for having preserved to her the most beautiful and interesting of her historical monuments."

Our guide took us through the Generalife first. Just as one would walk through the garden of a house before entering to see its interior so we explored the Generalife, the gardens of the Alhambra, before entering the castle.

Here is a place that would have gladdened the heart of Luther Burbank. Here the Moors would enjoy to the utmost their three loves of life. Here they played with water and made it perform a thousand sparkling duties for their enjoyment. An archway of water here, a sparkling fountain there.

In every appropriate nook and corner we find water rushing and gurgling. Water sparkling with all the brilliance of a diamond. And one wonders where it all comes from. Surely only master engineers could invent the system that could make water perform so many and varied delightful tricks.

On each side, like deep grooved banisters, continuing to the very top of a series of steps that takes one high above the gardens of the Generalife, comes rushing the ice cold water from the melted snow of the Sierra Nevada mountains to cool the air and supply the waters that play with such fascinating beauty through this magnificent garden.

It was here, in the Generalife, that the Moorish kings came to enjoy the refreshments of their gardens, and found relief from the heat during the summer months.

THE COURT OF THE LIONS IN THE ALHAMBRA.

SPAIN: A LAND BLIGHTED BY RELIGION

A Moorish poet has described the Generalife as "so many pearls set in a bed of Emeralds."

But perhaps the best description of the Generalife is the Arabic inscription on the walls. It reads: "How beauteous is this garden; where the flowers of the earth vie with the stars of heaven. What can compare with the vase of yon alabaster fountain filled with crystal water! nothing but the moon in her fullness, shining in the midst of an unclouded sky."

Washington Irving tells of having sat for hours inhaling the sweetness of this garden.

If the gardens of the Generalife beggar description, how inadequate is language in describing the Alhambra itself. And if I thought for one moment that I was going to try and describe my visit to the Alhambra I possibly would still be in Spain.

No superficial description can do justice to this place.

To describe the Alhambra properly one must live in it and be a part of it; one must study it and one must take time to do it. The best that one can do on a short visit to the Alhambra, and even this only partially, is to grasp the magnificence of the place and a sense of appreciation for the masters who built it.

Washington Irving spent some time at the Alhambra and perhaps from him we can get some idea of the grandest palace that the Moors built in Spain.

Crossing the threshold is as if one were transported by a magic wand into an oriental realm and scenes of an Arabian story.

The effect is so much the greater because the unpre-

[44]

tentious exterior is in marked contrast to the delicate beauty and rare charm of the interior. This seems to be part of the Moorish culture. An austere plainness marks the exterior of their houses, while within can be found unparalleled splendor.

"We found ourselves," says Washington Irving, "in a vast patio or court, one hundred and fifty feet in length, and upwards of eighty feet in breadth, paved with white marble, and decorated at each end with light Moorish peristyles, one of which is supported by an elegant gallery of fretted architecture. Along the moulding of the cornices and on various parts of the walls were escutcheons and ciphers, and Cufic and Arabic characters in high relief, repeating the pious mottoes of the Moslem monarchs, the builders of the Alhambra, or extolling their grandeur and munificence. Along the center of the court extended an immense basin or tank (estanque), a hundred and twenty-four feet in length, twenty-seven in breadth, and five in depth, receiving its water from two marble vases. Hence it is called the Court of the Alberca (from *alBerkah,* the Arabic for pond or tank). Great numbers of gold fish were to be seen gleaming through the waters of the basin, and it was bordered by hedges of roses.

"Passing from the Court of the Alberca under a Moorish archway, we entered the renowned Court of Lions. No part of the edifice gives a more complete idea of its original beauty than this, for none has suffered so little from the ravages of time. The alabaster basins still shed their diamond drops."

SPAIN: A LAND BLIGHTED BY RELIGION

The Moors, like the Jews, took literally the provision of the second commandment and made no images and produced no likenesses of the things of the earth. For that reason there have been many tales told of the reason for the existence of the twelve lions in this court of the Alhambra. Some say that the lions were so perfect that even the Moors could not see them destroyed. But that is not true. The lions are rank pieces of sculpture and are unworthy to stand in the Alhambra. The more probable reason for their existence is that they were made by a Christian captive and for some unknown reason placed in this court. One does not have to have a trained eye for perfection and symmetry to recognize instantly their marring effect. Another defect of this court is that it is laid out in flower beds instead of appropriate pavement of marble. This alteration, it is said, is an instance of bad taste made by the French when in possession of Granada.

But I must return to Washington Irving to continue his description.

"Round the four sides of the court are light Arabian arcades of open filigree work, supported by slender pillars of white marble, which it is supposed were originally gilded. The architecture, like that in most parts of the interior of the palace, is characterized by elegance rather than grandeur, bespeaking a delicate and graceful taste, and a disposition to indolent enjoyment. When one looks upon the fairy traces of the peristyles, and apparently fragile fretwork of the walls, it is difficult to believe that so much has survived the wear and tear of centuries, the shocks of the earthquakes, the violence of war, and the quiet, though no less baneful, pilferings of the tasteful traveler; it is almost sufficient to excuse the popular tradition, that the whole is protected by a magic charm.

"On one side of the court a rich portal opens into the Hall of the Abencerrages; so-called from the gallant cavaliers of that illustrious line who were here perfidiously massacred. Immediately opposite the Hall of the Abencerrages, a portal, richly adorned, leads into a hall of less tragical associations. It is light and lofty, exquisitely graceful in its architecture, paved with white marble, and bears the suggestive name of the Hall of the Two Sisters."

The popular reason for this being called the Hall of the Two Sisters is due to the fact that in it are two enormous slabs of alabaster, which lie side by side and are identical in all their beauty and perfection. Others claim the reason for its name is due to twin Moorish beauties—the third of the Moorish loves—part of the royal harem, which once graced this hall.

"On each side of this hall are recesses or alcoves for ottomans and couches, on which the voluptuous lords of the Alhambra indulged in that dreamy repose so dear to the Orientalists. A cupola or lantern admits a tempered light from above and a free circulation of air; while on one side is heard the refreshing sound of waters from the fountain of the lions, and on the other side the soft splash from the basin in the garden of Lindaraxa.

"It is impossible to contemplate this scene," says Irving, "so perfectly Oriental, without feeling the early association of Arabian romance, and almost expecting to see the white arm of some mysterious princess beckoning from the gallery or some dark eye sparkling through the lattice."

Irving continues: "An abundant supply of water, brought from the mountains by old Moorish aqueducts, circulated throughout the palace, supplying its baths and fishpools, sparkling in jets within its halls or murmuring in channels along the marble pavements. When it had paid its tribute to the royal pile, and visited its gardens and parterres, it flowed down the long avenue leading to the city, trickling rills, gushing in fountains, and maintaining a perpetual verdure in those groves that embower and beautify the whole hill of the Alhambra."

There is no limit to the description that one could write about the Alhambra, but to fail to mention the Hall of the Ambassadors would be unforgivable.

"It is thirty-seven feet square and fifty feet high, and still bears the traces of its past magnificence. Its ceilings were cedar and vermilion with the rich gildings and brilliants tints of the Moorish pencil.

"On three sides of the Hall of the Ambassadors are windows cut through the immense thickness of the walls and commanding extensive prospects. The balcony of the central window especially looks down upon the verdant valley of the Darro, with its walls, its groves and gardens. To the left, it enjoys a distinct prospect of the Vega; while directly in front rises the rival heights of the Albaycin, with its medley of streets, and terraces, and gardens and once crowned by a fortress that vied in power with the Alhambra."

It was from one of these windows that Isabella watched Columbus walk away after being refused ships and men for his voyage across the ocean. And as she saw him plodding his way with a determination to seek help from France, she sent messengers running to him with the good news that she had agreed to comply with his request. And standing in this same room, two generations later looking forth upon the commanding scenery it affords, Charles the Fifth exclaimed: "Ill-fated the man who lost all this."

And when Boabdil, the last of the Moorish kings, faced inevitable defeat and the loss of this irreplaceable castle, and with it the realization of the loss of all the power and glory and splendor of the civilization that they had built, no wonder he began to weep, only to be remonstrated by his mother with these words: "You do well," she said, "to weep as a woman over what you could not defend as a man."

The spot where this occurred is called *La Cuesta de las Lagrimas* (the hill of tears) and a little beyond is a place denominated *el ultimo suspiro del Moro* (the last sign of the Moor), for it was here that Boabdil looked back and bid farewell forever to the most enchanting building that was ever fashioned by the hands of man. One does not have to be a king to leave the Alhambra with a sigh. A feeling of depression comes over you when you realize that the people who had really brought the splendor and glory to Spain had been driven out, dis-

SPAIN: A LAND BLIGHTED BY RELIGION

persed, and practically annihilated; the material treasures they had left confiscated, and the culture and learning that they had developed destroyed.

I am again constrained to quote Washington Irving as a summary of who the Moors were and their accomplishments while in Spain.

He says: "Repelled within the limits of the Pyrenees, the mixed hordes of Asia and Africa, that formed this great irruption, gave up the Moslem principle of conquest, and sought to establish in Spain a peaceful and permanent dominion. As conquerors, their heroism was only equalled by their moderation; and in both, for a time they excelled the nations with whom they contended. Severed from their homes, they loved the land given them as they supposed by Allah, and strove to embellish it with everything that could administer to the happiness of man. Laying the foundation of their power in a system of wise and equitable laws, diligently cultivating the arts and sciences, and promoting agriculture, manufactures, and commerce, they gradually formed an empire unrivalled for its prosperity by any of the empires of Christendom; and diligently drawing round them the graces and refinements which marked the Arabian empire in the East, at the time of its greatest civilization, they diffused the light of Oriental knowledge through the western regions of benighted Europe.

"The cities of Arabian Spain became the resort of Christian artisans, to instruct themselves in the useful arts. The universities of Toledo, Cordova, Seville and Granada were sought by the pale student from other

THE HALL OF JUSTICE IN THE ALHAMBRA.

SPAIN: A LAND BLIGHTED BY RELIGION

lands to acquaint himself with the sciences of the Arabs and the treasured lore of antiquity; the lovers of the gay science resorted to Cordova and Granada, to imbibe the poetry and music of the East; and the steel-clad warriors of the North hastened thither to accomplish themselves in the graceful exercises and courteous usages of chivalry.

"If the Moslem monuments in Spain, if the Mosque of Cordova, the Alcazar of Seville, and the Alhambra of Granada, still bear inscriptions fondly boasting of the power and permanency of their dominion, can the boast be derided as arrogant and vain?"

I am not militaristic, but there is a grave lesson for preparedness in the destruction and expulsion of the Moors from Spain. While fully prepared for defense, no tribe, no nation, was the equal to the courageous and dashing Moor. It was only after he felt himself secure; only after he had settled down to the pursuits of peace, the cultivation of knowledge, the development of science, the establishment of industry, the building of homes, the contentment of family life, and the happiness of his people that any attempt was made to attack him. And were it not for the duplicity of the Visigoths under their Catholic Kings, the Moors would not only have remained to the glory of Spain but it is quite probable that today the entire world would be a thousand years advanced in the progress of science and the development and happiness of mankind.

There was only one other thing of interest for us to see before leaving Granada and that was the tomb of Isabella and Ferdinand. We looked with contempt upon the tomb of these two fanatical rulers whose Catholicism was responsible for the disaster that overtook the Spain of Romance, of Love, and of Life.

I consider the period of Catholicism which prevailed in the Spain of Isabella and Ferdinand an intellectual black plague from which the peoples of this earth have not yet fully recovered.

No one should forget the year 1492, not because in that year Columbus set sail to discover America, but because in 1492 Granada was captured, the Alhambra converted into a Catholic shrine, and the most tragic disaster then befell the human race.

Theology triumphed over philosophy; superstition over knowledge; prejudice and bigotry exultantly raised the cross with the fanatical cry of "Death to the infidels."

It took over four hundred years before the spell of this mad superstition was finally lifted.

MALAGA

AGAIN we are leaving Cordova at six o'clock in the morning. Our destination is Malaga. This city of the Mediterranean is famous for its raisins, its wine and its sunshine. Malaga boasts of having only twenty-nine rainy days in the year.

Waiting at a Spanish railroad station for a train to arrive from another city is an experience that you can only get in Spain. Finally the train did come. A stationman announced that the incoming train was going to Malaga. We boarded it with all of our baggage, and just as the train started an English-speaking passenger, overhearing our conversation, politely told us that the train *we were on* was *not* going to Malaga.

One can imagine our consternation. I jumped off the train and in perfectly good English I asked every stationman and conductor whether this train was going to Malaga and of course not one could understand what I was saying. Finally the conductor of the sleeping car told us that the *train* was going to Malaga but not the *car* in which we were seated. After some difficulty, and with a great deal of relief, we moved our baggage to the car that was going to Malaga.

One would have to go a long distance and travel

through many countries before one would find more beautiful scenery than that which we saw on our way to this celebrated Mediterranean city.

We stopped at the Caleta Palace Hotel, directly on the shore of the Mediterranean. The playful splashing of the waters against the rocks, the inimitable blue of the sea, the balmy sunshine, and a poet like Omar Khayyam might well speak of "a paradise enow."

Along the Mediterranean are the official homes of the Consuls of the different countries. And to my amazement I found one with the name "Villa Jesus" carved in the iron on the gate.

But a walk through the little city of Malaga tells quite a different story.

One cannot help but feel deeply for the people of this once priest-robbed country. Beggars are everywhere. Abject poverty seems to be the lot of the majority of the people. Bedraggled mothers are seen carrying children that are blind or crippled; some with sore eyes or blotched faces. Children, whose tiny noses are sore and bleeding from the constant dripping of the mucus, dog your steps pleading for alms. Their clothes are a little better than rags. It will take a long time to emancipate these people from the superstition that has enslaved them. Even the better dressed girls and women are seen on their way to mass carrying their little testaments and rosaries. A trip through the business section of the city reveals the reason for the people's condition. Windows are still filled with crucifixes and with statues of Mary and Jesus. Essential merchandise is scarce. A pair of

SPAIN: A LAND BLIGHTED BY RELIGION

shoes is a luxury. A combination cardboard with a cloth top is the foot covering that the majority of the poor populace wear.

And it does not take long to discover the reason for it all. The church has actually robbed the country of every particle of its wealth. What the church left the state absorbed.

Previous to the recent revolution, it is said that you could not walk the streets without rubbing shoulders with some priest. The priests actually convinced the people that their lot in life was part of the divine plan! Is it any wonder that the people of this beautiful country have been reduced to a condition little better than serfdom?

MADRID

WE were to experience our first night on a sleeper on a Spanish railroad and at eight o'clock we boarded the train for Madrid. I was keenly desirous of visiting this world-famed city. Our train from Malaga to Madrid was two and one-half hours late, which was in perfect accord with an old Spanish custom. As we arrived at Madrid I could see through the window our friend, Mrs. Nurita Estrugo, waiting for us on the platform. This meeting emphasizes how rapidly science is bringing the peoples of the earth closer together. My friendship with Jose Estrugo began with his reading "The Bible Unmasked" in Brazil.

For a moment we thought we were no longer in Spain. Here was a modern railroad station with pulsating activity. And what a great relief it is to meet someone you know and who also knows the language of the country you are visiting to relieve you of the difficulty of trying to tell your porter where you want to go. Riding from the station to the hotel I judged Madrid to be a little New York. I don't think my impression was too far wrong. Here the new and the old Spain meet and here also meet the strangers who visit Spain. Madrid is modern Spain. From here go forth the ideas that permeate the whole country. Here the radical and the conservative; the aristocrat and the peon; the banker and the laborer; the wealthy and the poor; the intellectual and the superstitious meet. Madrid is the vortex in which the great struggle of what Spain is to be is now going on. From what I saw, there is no doubt about the outcome. *Anticlericalism is in the ascendancy.* Spain is looking forward to a new era. Hardly a day passes without a special article, generally on the front page in the leading newspapers in two and three column headlines, attacking the clergy and particularly the Jesuits.

One particular article characterized the Jesuits as intruders and said that the people were happy that they had been expelled. It said that not a voice was raised in their defense. It told how a Jesuit would come uninvited to a home, and once securely inside, how difficult it was to get rid of him. He would cloak himself with the authority of the master of the house and regulate the household's activity to suit his convenience. Even the intimate relations of the family were subject to his whims and caprices. He was condemned as a parasite and as a corrupter of morals. His departure from a home would be celebrated with much relief and joy. No invitation was ever extended twice to a Jesuit. One visit was all that a family could stand.

Another article denounced the so-called charitable organizations of the church. The article demanded a thorough investigation and an accounting. The churches were openly accused of diverting money that had been contributed for a specific charitable purpose to their own selfish ends.

When the present government secularized the schools, the old ladies of the church and the members of the old aristocracy paraded the streets of Madrid with banners bearing words of horrified indignation at the dethronement of Jesus in the class-rooms. They mourned that their children were being deprived of the saving grace of Jesus. They were hooted and pelted by the crowds that lined the sidewalks. And when this once exclusively and completely Catholic nation became cognizant of what the Church and her clergy had done they became infuriated and fired the churches and convents.

If the men from the fire department answered the call they refused to put out the fire for fear of the fury of the mob. They played the water upon the surrounding buildings to prevent the fire from spreading.

An appeal was made to the leader of the State troops who at the same time was a member of the new parliament to prevent further destruction of church property, but he said that to use his men to prevent the firing of the churches would precipitate a riot with the inevitable result of bloodshed, and as for himself, he would rather see every church and convent burnt to the ground than to have one republican life lost! It was the intervention of freethinking leaders of the republic that prevented complete destruction of the church edifices.

In no country that we visited were the clergy held in greater contempt. They are looked upon as symbols and representatives of a brutally callous and thieving organization.

But the battle has not been won and will not be won until religion as a political power has been completely broken and disintegrated. The Jesuits were expelled once before from Spain; they know the art of waiting and the tendency of the people to forget. But if the spirit of the present generation of Spaniards prevail, the Jesuits will be disappointed this time. Unless the forward-looking people of the world are to be keenly disappointed, the king and the priest will never again gain a foothold on the soil of Spain.

Fernando de Los Rios

One of my first pleasures in Madrid was meeting Fernando de Los Rios, the Minister of Public Instruction. I came to him with a letter of introduction from the Spanish Embassy in Washington. Only one visit was necessary to convince me that Fernando de Los Rios was a man of tremendous force in the new government. And he was properly placed as Minister of Public Instruction. It is in the channels of the Public Schools of Spain that her future rests, and no small measure of her success will be due to the man who is now guiding the education of her youth.

And what do you suppose are the charges that the church has brought against this man? One is that he believes in religious liberty, the other is that he personally went to the Sephardic Jews, whose ancestors were expelled from Spain and who now live in Algiers, and who still speak the Spanish language and still observe the customs of their native land, and asked them to return to Spain so that the present government could, in a measure, wipe out the blot that still stains the history of his country for the cruel expulsion of their ancestors.

The clergy attribute these "treasonable acts" on the part of Fernando de Los Rios to the blood of his "Jewish" ancestors!

R. Cansino-Assens

One of the ablest literary men in Spain; and one of the most prodigious writers is R. Cansino-Assens, the literary editor of *La Libertad*. Not only is he an author of great repute himself, but is perhaps Spain's best translator. He can translate into Spanish, and beautiful Spanish too, from eight or ten different languages. One of the most peculiar traits about him is that he cannot speak a word of any language other than Spanish; and yet he can translate from Russian with the same ease that he does from English.

Much to my surprise I found Cansinos taking great pride from his Jewish ancestry. In fact, so keenly does he feel his kinship with the Jews, that he is the author of several important books dealing with the Jewish customs in Spain before their expulsion. And this is the strange thing. His own sister is so devoutedly Catholic that she refuses to live in the same apartment with him.

SPAIN: A LAND BLIGHTED BY RELIGION

Ogier Preteceille

He is the foreign editor of *Luz*. I was in the office of this newspaper, keeping an appointment with Mr. Preteceille when the news was flashed over the world telling of the tragedy of the kidnapping of the Lindbergh baby. Preteceille was born in France and was educated to be a priest. He came home one day from school and told his father that he could no longer apply himself to the study of religion and that he considered it a great fraud. His father was so incensed that he ordered him from his house and told him not to return until he was ready to resume his studies. It was war time. Some suggested that he go to England. But he feared that he would be returned to France and forced to enter the army. Someone suggested that he go to Spain. There he was told that he would be in a neutral country and at the same time would have an opportunity to study a new language. This he did. He also found a wife in Valencia. And the second time that I saw him was at his lovely little home, with his two beautiful daughters. He insisted that we visit him so we could have a dish of Spanish rice as cooked by his wife in the real Valencian style.

He told me that after the war he did return home, only, however, for a visit, and paid a terrible penalty for leaving. His mother had died. I forgot to tell you that I had difficulty in pronouncing his name. He told me that in French it was pronounced *Pray-t'-sayya,* in Spanish *Pre-te-silla,* but his American friends call him *Pretty*

MADRID. THE ENTRANCE MARCH OF THE BULL-FIGHTERS IN THE ARENA.

silly. To make certain that I would not make a mistake I called him *Ogier*.

But I cannot begin to tell you of all the people I met in Madrid, because then my narrative would be entirely too long. However, I will mention only one more. That is Ramon J. Sender. He is a young writer of great promise. It is his articles that are appearing in the press throughout Spain, attacking the church with such devastating logic. If he continues unabated he will become one of the outstanding writers in Spain.

My First Bullfight

In Madrid I saw my first bullfight; it undoubtedly will be my last. It was the first bullfight of the season too. The arena is built very much like our baseball parks. Although there was a chill wind in the air and dark clouds were overhead, there was nevertheless a goodly crowd present. And seated near us were a group of young girls still in their teens. And they were pretty too. If they were specimens of the typical Spanish girl, then no wonder they have inspired fervent love songs. But somehow I thought they were out of place at a bullfight; but "handsome is as handsome does", and if they could find enjoyment and pleasurable excitement at a bullfight, their pretty faces were only a mask for their sadism.

We hear the strains of martial music and we see marching across the field the toreadors and banderilleros who are going to engage the bulls in combat. Following them are picadors mounted upon horseback. And then I see four horses pulling a rather peculiarly constructed device. For a moment I thought it was to smooth the surface of the ring; just as is done at our baseball parks so the ball will roll smoothly across the field. But this instrument had an altogether different use, and as I had never seen a bullfight before I did not know what it would be used for until I saw it in operation. It is to drag the bull off the field after he has been killed.

The bullfight that I saw in Madrid is the cruelest and most unsportsmanlike contest that I have ever seen. The bull has absolutely no chance whatsoever. He is doomed the moment he enters the arena. And I will tell you frankly that my sympathy was with the bull. To torment and torture an animal merely for enjoyment that one gets from it is a sport that is not to my liking. If we must kill for food let us do it in the quickest and least painful method. But to torment, torture and kill for the pleasure that one gets from it is a combination of savagery, barbarism and brutality that man should be ashamed even to countenance.

Even though Catholicism, as taught in Spain, teaches its adherents that animals have no souls, and were put on earth for man's pleasure, nevertheless that cannot justify this unwarranted butchery of these fine animal specimens.

I was glad to learn that under the new régime there is a concerted effort on foot to abolish this inhuman sport.

SPAIN: A LAND BLIGHTED BY RELIGION

The Prado

I visited the Prado which, next to the Louvre in Paris, is considered the finest art gallery in the world. I visited the Prado with great expectations. I had remembered reading in Lecky's "Rationalism in Europe" of a remarkable painting of an Inquisitorial scene by a contemporary artist.

On my first visit there I made inquiries concerning it, but no one seemed to know where it was; in fact, I was told that no such picture existed and it certainly was not in the Prado.

During the visit, however, in search of the picture, I came across an artist by the name of Gomez. I asked him about it and the only pictures concerning the inquisition that were to his knowledge in the Prado were the two Berreguettes. These he showed me, but neither one was the picture I had in mind. Finally after much talk he took me over to the stairway in a far and not much frequented corner of the building and there against the wall, covering it in its entirety, was this tremendous canvas. It is twelve feet high by eighteen feet long. To be properly placed it should be against a wall with at least a five foot margin all around it. And the pity of it all is that about 12 inches had been cut off the picture in order that it might hang within the space where we found it. Mr. Gomez bemoaned this fact, stating that they cut part of the picture with the same unconcern with which they burnt the victims.

The importance and value of this picture lies in the

THE PAINTING BY FRANCESCO RIZZI OF AN INQUISITION AUTO-DA-FÉ.

SPAIN: A LAND BLIGHTED BY RELIGION

fact that it is the only authentic, contemporary painting of the Inquisition, with the faces of the characters as they actually appeared at the time of the Auto da fé.

The painting was made by a well-known artist of his day by the name of Francesco Rizzi. As valuable as this picture is in itself, it becomes so much more precious because the Church in Spain has systematically and deliberately destroyed everything they could that pertained to the Inquisition.

Let me quote Lecky's note of the description of this picture. . . .

"It represents the execution, or rather the procession to the stake, of a number of Jews and Jewesses who were burnt in 1680 at Madrid, during the fêtes that followed the marriage of Charles II., and before the king, his bride, the court and the clergy of Madrid. The great square was arranged like a theatre, and thronged with ladies in court dress; the king sat on an elevated platform surrounded by the chief members of the aristocracy, and Bishop Valdares, the Inquisitor-General, presided over the scene. The painter of this very remarkable picture which is in the gallery of Madrid was Francesco Rizzi, who died in 1685. . . . The picture is very curious from its representation of the attire of the condemned and of the penitent. . . . Among the victims in 1860 was a Jewish girl, not 17, whose singular beauty struck all who saw her with admiration. As she passed to the stake, she cried to the queen, 'Great queen, is not your presence able to bring me some comfort under my misery? Consider my youth, and that I am condemned for a religion which I have sucked in with my mother's milk.' The queen turned away her eyes."

Whether Lecky ever saw this painting or not I do not know, but if he had, I am sure he would have made mention of the scene which is depicted at the bottom of the canvas.

There is a victim, with his tongue ripped out, being led away, to be burnt, in company with several priests, one of whom is trying to press a crucifix to his bleeding lips.

I visited the Plaza Major, the square in which the scene of the picture was laid, and the buildings and surroundings are easily recognizable.

The Prado is the treasure house of the paintings of Velasquez and Goya, the two greatest of Spanish artists, as well as those of el Greco and Murillo.

Goya painted a victim of the Inquisition being garroted in the public square. Many of his paintings, depicting scenes of hallucinations, were made to represent the unbalancing of the mind by religious dogma. There is this story current about Goya throughout Spain. He was called upon to paint a picture in which Mary and Elizabeth were two of the leading characters. He refused to do the work, because he said he was not religious and could not execute the work properly. He was told that he must do the painting or be subjected to the wrath of the church. With reluctance he agreed. But he took as his models for both Mary and Elizabeth the two must notorious prostitutes in Madrid. It is their faces that he painted in this picture for the church, that represent the two most sacred female characters of the New Testament.

ESCORIAL

NO one who goes to Spain and visits the Mezquita in Cordova, the Alcazar in Seville and the Alhambra in Granada should fail to visit the Escorial. No, not because it is like the places just mentioned—on the contrary—because it is so different.

The Escorial was built by a madman. It was built by a religiously insane king, and offers a fine example of the difference between the philosophy of the Moors and the religion of the Christians. The Moors built for the living; the Christians for the dead. One believed in enjoying this life, the other in preparing for death. One "took the cash and let the credit go", and the other believed in making himself as miserable as possible while on earth, so he could be resurrected and enjoy eternal bliss in the paradise to come; the more you suffer here the less you will suffer hereafter was his religious doctrine. Compare the Escorial with the Alhambra and then decide which philosophy you prefer to follow.

The Escorial was built by King Philip II. And in building the Escorial he built his bedroom adjoining the Cathedral, so when he was too ill to get out of bed he could open the door of his room and watch Mass being said. He also built a special seat in the Cathedral adjoin-

SPAIN: A LAND BLIGHTED BY RELIGION

ing the door of his bedroom so when he was able to get out of bed it would not be too difficult for him to enter the church.

I wonder if Philip ever gave any thought to the idea that, if his religion was unable to cure his illness, how utterly impossible it was to preserve his soul. He could never have been convinced of such a premise because he believed that sickness was sent by God as a punishment for sin, and the only way to effect a cure was to pray for the forgiveness of his sinful acts.

I sat in Philip's seat in the Cathedral and my only regret was that he was not present so he could hear what I thought of him and his insane Escorial. With the marble that the Moors took from the Sierra Nevada Mountains they built beautiful public baths, adorned their homes with marble walks, marble stairways and marble bannisters. The marble that Philip took from the mountains of his country he made into coffins. He made enough coffins for all the kings of Spain, for all the relatives of the kings, and for all the children of all the relatives of the kings. He made coffins, and coffins, and coffins. The Escorial is a gigantic graveyard. The most appropriate monument that could be erected to his memory would be a coffin. He should have adopted the skull and cross bones for the coat of arms of his kingdom. Philip II of Spain should be made the patron saint of the undertakers.

Until the government's decree regarding religious institutions is put into effect, the Escorial is still used as a seminary. There I saw young priests walking up and

THE ESCORIAL, ANCESTRAL HOME OF THE SPANISH KINGS.

down mumbling to themselves Biblical quotations, which brought to my mind these words:

> "The learned block-heads'
>   ignorantly read,
> With loads of learned
>   lumber in their heads."

Take this advice: Do not visit the Escorial on your honeymoon. For no matter how full of joy you are, or bubbling over with happiness, the Escorial will have a tremendously depressing effect upon you.

VALLADOLID

VALLADOLID was once the capital of Spain. That it is no longer the center of governmental activity is quite evident to anyone who visits it. That it is the remains and ruins of a once splendid city adds to the tragedy of the glory that once was Spain.

One can imagine this city in the days of Cervantes. It must have been the Mecca where the artistic and the intellectual mingled together. I visited Cervantes' home, and I walked through what is left of the gardens. It is here that the literary genius of Spain gave to the world Don Quixote. I visited the palace of Cardinal Mendoza, which has since been converted into a museum. With the exception of the painting showing Antonio Perez after being tortured by the Inquisition, it is truly a museum of curiosities. Here the frightful statues of Saints and Madonnas are stored like so much furniture. One can imagine the effect of these hideous-faced statues upon the credulous and superstitious, especially when intensified by the lurid discourses of the viciously minded priests. Many "sacred" relics are preserved here. Relics however that are no longer effective. Here are also stored the statues and floats mounted on wheels which are used in the annual parades at Easter time.

Their crudity, however, I am sure, did not detract from their effectiveness in instilling hatred in the minds of the people who watched these "sacred" figures pass through the streets in solemn procession led by priests. The purpose of these floats was to intensify the religion of the people by arousing their hatred for those who "killed their Lord", so their contributions to wipe out the Jews would be large and numerous.

To eradicate the prejudice and hatred instilled by these processions the new government has issued a decree prohibiting them. When I was in Valladolid the priests and their supporters were quite incensed because they were unable to continue this vicious trade. Everything that they could do to embarrass the government in their program of reconstruction was done, and done with a vengeance.

Here I found the priests well groomed. Their garments were fresh and new, their hats of the finest beaver. They formed a distinct contrast to the mass of people. The people were ill-clad, and on display in the shops was the cheapest merchandise.

In Valladolid I got some understanding of the charge made by the Mexican government that the priests were corrupting the community in which they lived and to prevent the complete demoralization of family life they were compelled to enact a law limiting the number of priests to but one to each one hundred thousand population. Perhaps Spain will follow Mexico in this respect and some day the New Spain will do something to curb these corrupters of morals.

VALLADOLID. THE COURTYARD IN WHICH ARE STORED FLOATS FORMERLY USED IN RELIGIOUS PROCESSIONS.

SPAIN: A LAND BLIGHTED BY RELIGION

In the Palace of Justice at Valladolid, which was afterwards used as an Inquisitorial chamber, Isabella and Ferdinand were married. A white marble plaque marks the spot. Judging from the results of this marriage and its influence upon human progress a black crepe of mourning should symbolize this event. The building today, however, is used for government archives.

I was extremely anxious to secure all the data available concerning the Inquisition in Spain, and when I visited this building I inquired of the librarian in charge if he could supply me with any information of that institution. When I stressed the fact that I was interested in the methods of torture and the instruments used, he looked at me with a whimsical smile and said that if anyone thought that instruments of torture were used during the Inquisition it was a "fantasy". *His remarks gave me the first actual evidence of the fact that the Catholic Church in Spain has been systematically destroying all evidence procurable dealing with this religious reign of terror.* Now I can understand why it is almost impossible to secure a single instrument of torture in Spain, and why no public museum has a single item. Once the church took pride in the Inquisition, but now, since the entire civilized world has condemned it, the church is slyly seeking to destroy the evidence of its once frightful existence.

PANORAMIC VIEW OF TOLEDO.

TOLEDO

IN company with Mr. and Mrs. Preteceille and with Mr. and Mrs. Estrugo we left Madrid on a beautiful Sunday morning to spend a day at Toledo. Toledo is one of the most famous cities of Spain. When the Moors ruled this beautiful country, Toledo was noted not only for its beautiful castles and great educational institutions, but also for its intense commercial activity and the manufacture of the finest steel that the world had ever known. One's admiration continually increases for the Moors when one analyzes the perfect judgment they used in selecting the places for their cities.

Upon a high elevation, surrounded by the River Tagus, with a beautiful gorge below, Toledo was built.

Here we saw some of the magnificent Toledo work, the art of which is another legacy left by the Moors. This beautiful work, made with a hammer and a thread of gold is a marvelous example of the artistic development of these dark-skinned people.

However, the Toledo scale which we found in the hotel where we had a most delicious meal was made in Toledo, Ohio.

In Toledo I saw the most beautiful synagogue that

THE CATHEDRAL OF TOLEDO.

SPAIN: A LAND BLIGHTED BY RELIGION

was ever built. Although a thousand years old and used for a Christian church for more than 400 years, it still bears the imprint of the genius of the Moorish builders. There is an unmistakable kinship between the synagogue and the Alhambra.

I saw the Cathedral of Toledo with hundreds of iron shackles fastened to the front of the church, which were used to punish the victims of the creed the cathedral represents.

On Sunday this cathedral is something like a circus. You pay a substantial admission to enter. Once inside you go from curiosity to curiosity. Here is a conglomeration of all silly and worthless things of the church as well as valuable things put to useless purposes. In one room I saw cloaks worn by the different cardinals of Spain, and most noteworthy of all was the one worn by Cardinal Mendoza. It was covered entirely with matchless pearls. The cost that the poor deluded fools paid for these thousands of precious stones probably can never be computed. Room after room is filled with the travesties that religion has produced. Different shrines line the walls of the immense cathedral and one sight touched my heart. I saw an old bedraggled woman, kneel before a shrine, on the walls of which were many soot-colored letters and small celluloid arms and legs that were evidently used in making dolls. On inquiry I discovered that these things were put there by the relatives of those suffering from ailments of the limbs. Here prayers are said, and a box conveniently placed so contributions can be received. On this Sunday, I saw this old

SEVILLE. A COURT IN PILATE'S HOUSE.

SPAIN: A LAND BLIGHTED BY RELIGION

woman kneel, pray and drop a few coins into the box. Surely this woman could ill afford to part with any money that was needed for medical attention. After performing this duty she went to another shrine, enclosed within an iron railing and again prayed fervently. This shrine contained a "sacred" relic. I too went to the shrine, because I was anxious to see the relic, but unfortunately my faith was not strong enough!

I saw the only remaining Mosque in Toledo. It was small and rapidly nearing destruction.

And then I thought of what Toledo was before its capture by the Christians.

When Toledo was under the Moorish kingdom all sects lived in perfect harmony. The Moors, the Jews and the Christians practiced their religion without the slightest molestation. Never once did they persecute for opinion's sake. Religious toleration was part and parcel of their political philosophy.

But what a change took place when Christianity gained control of Toledo. Not only was no other religious opinion tolerated, but expulsion and death were the penalties imposed upon unbelief. Intolerance and bigotry became the dominating factors of their government. The great secular institutions of learning founded by the Moors, which were the admiration of all Europe, were converted into seminaries to manufacture priests.

The scientific pursuit of knowledge was replaced by the never-to-be questioned precepts of the Bible.

The dictionaries, encyclopedias, and the results of scientific researches of a thousand years were blindly and fanatically destroyed, never to be recovered.

Toledo today is a pitiful reminder of what it was. However, it should be preserved that it may stand as a perpetual monument to the toleration of the Moors.

BARCELONA

WHEN we boarded the train at Madrid and arrived the next morning, on time, at Barcelona, it upset an old Spanish custom.

Approaching Barcelona from the shore of the picturesque Mediterranean, seeing in the distance the smoke whirling from a thousand chimneys, you immediately feel the presence of a thriving European community, pulsating with the life of a modern city.

And strange as it may seem, Barcelona is called the city of the future, and if the cities of the future are as pretty as Barcelona, then indeed the earth will become a garden spot. I did not go to Barcelona for the purpose of judging its beauty, but if the rest of the city equalled in beauty and good taste the Paseo de Gracia where our hotel was situated, the rest of the world might copy the plan of this Catalonian city without the slightest misgiving.

From the balcony of our room a complete panorama opened before us. Looking to the south I saw the blue waters of the Mediterranean; to the north the majestic mountain of Tibidabo.

The world has sung the praises of the Avenue Des Champs Elysées in Paris, but in my opinion the Paseo

BARCELONA

de Gracia in Barcelona possesses a beauty and charm that surpasses the famous Parisian thoroughfare.

In Barcelona is one of the most unusual sights I have seen in any city. There in the evening, in the silver birch trees that line the main business thoroughfare, thousands upon thousands of birds sleep all night. The birds are of the same color as the leaves, making it almost impossible for one to distinguish between them. The birds begin to settle on the trees at dusk, and their chirping is one continuous chatter that does not subside until sleep overtakes them. They seem like a big family that has come together to talk over the day's labor. The only sight similar to this that I can remember is the thousands of sparrows that inhabit the trees in Washington, directly in front of the Post Office building. However, there was a marked difference between the birds in Barcelona and those in Washington.

In Washington the sparrows were the common variety and remained continuously in and around the trees, disturbing the entire area with their chirping. Those in Barcelona were of a light gray color and only inhabited the trees in the evening. During the day the limbs of the trees were bare and not a single bird was to be seen.

In Barcelona I met Mr. Pedro Soler, and meeting Mr. Soler in Barcelona is proof of how small the earth really is and how the barriers between people are rapidly breaking down. Mr. Soler remembered me from New York. He was even one of the few who were present at the meeting when I was elected President of the Freethinkers Society. He even remembered the words of a

SPAIN: A LAND BLIGHTED BY RELIGION

statement I made at this meeting. He told me that I said that there were thousands of men and women in New York who were Freethinkers and who would become members of the organization if they only knew of its existence. He said my prophecy had come true.

He put himself and his car at our disposal and was our constant companion in Barcelona, the city of his birth.

He is thorough-going in his Freethought and never loses an opportunity to attack the church. It was through his efforts that a Spanish publisher was secured for *The Bible Unmasked.*

On a Sunday morning we visited the Miramer, which overlooks the Mediterranean, affording as beautiful a sight of the city below as one can imagine. That evening Mr. Soler accompanied us to the top of Mount Tibidabo, and there we saw Barcelona at night with its myriad of electric lights aglow, making the city glitter like a sea of diamonds. Barcelona has everything that a city requires. It has the sea, the country, mountains and forest; with a climate that is ideal. No wonder it is a beautiful city.

The Catalonians feel a nearer kinship to the French and the rest of Europe than they do to the Spaniard. In fact they claim that the anti-religious movement started in Barcelona and spread through Spain. So determined are they to free themselves from the yoke of the church and king that no matter what the rest of Spain might do regarding the return of these two parasites of society the Catalonians will never tolerate their return.

I had the pleasure of meeting the mayor of this beautiful city, one of the brave men who suffered imprison-

FRANCISCO FERRER AND FOUR COMPANIONS WHO WERE EXECUTED IN 1908 FOR THEIR OPPOSITION TO THE CATHOLIC CHURCH.

ment for the ideals of a republican government. I was taken through the executive chamber, the department of justice and other rooms of the city's government.

I met the daughter of Francisco Ferrer, who had just returned to Spain to carry on the work left uncompleted by the assassination of her father.

I visited Montjuich, the fortress and prison where Ferrer was imprisoned and shot. It stands on top of a mountain overlooking the city and directly in front of the harbor approach of the Mediterranean.

It is the intention of the new government to abandon this fortress and permit the admirers of Ferrer to erect a monument to his memory upon the spot where he was shot. During my visit to the Mayor of Barcelona, one of my purposes was to secure permission from the city to permit the International Freethought Union to sponsor the erection of this monument in 1936 on the twenty-fifth anniversary of the assassination of Ferrer. This the mayor agreed to do and offered his complete and hearty cooperation.

I visited the various Freethought organizations in Barcelona who pledged their cooperation to this end. Let us hope that in a few years hence the Freethinkers of the world will meet in Barcelona to honor the Freethinker who did so much to liberate his country from the stranglehold of religion. Viva Francisco Ferrer!

The president of the Ferrer group of Freethinkers gave me a card with the pictures of Ferrer and the four others who were executed with him.

I was agreeably surprised at many things I saw in Bar-

BARCELONA

celona, but there was one thing in particular that I wanted to see.

The day following my arrival I asked the concierge at the hotel to direct the taxi cab driver to take me to the Inquisitorial Building. He looked at me surprised, and said that there was no such building in Barcelona. I told him that there was. Being unable to tell me where to find it, and unable to find its location in any of the city directories, I took it upon myself to find it. I asked taxi driver after taxi driver, all without success. Finally I told one to take me to the oldest cathedral in the city. This he did, and standing directly opposite was the Inquisitorial chamber, identical in every respect as it was built several hundreds of years ago. The only difference is that today it is used as an antique shop! I knew there was an Inquisitorial Building in Barcelona because I had seen a picture of it. I did not know, however, that directly above the entrance door I was to find the coat of arms of the Inquisition.

Directly adjoining this building was the prison and dungeon cells for the victims of the church. I lost no time in securing a photographer to get additional pictures of the building! And the photographer was once a choir boy in the cathedral! He told me that when he was in the choir, the priest, under a pledge of secrecy, took him and the other boys to a basement in the church and showed them the instruments of torture used upon victims!

It did not take long for the news of my discovery of the Inquisitorial Building to spread and many a resident

SPAIN: A LAND BLIGHTED BY RELIGION

of Barcelona made a special journey to see the building that they did not know existed.

To the members of the Freethinkers group I suggested that they make an application to have this building turned into a museum of religious articles dealing with the Inquisition and to secure the instruments of torture hidden in the basement of the adjoining cathedral!

There were many apologists for the church who said that the people did not want to remember such a painful period of history and I told them that I did not want the people to forget it.

Standing before this building, and reflecting on the horrors perpetrated by the Inquisition, these thoughts came to my mind.

In my travels through Spain I saw many buildings that were used as Inquisitorial chambers. In Seville I saw the crucifix which hung in the building of the Inquisition presided over by Torquemada. In Valladolid I saw the Palace of Justice, which was afterwards used as an inquisitorial chamber, where Isabella and Ferdinand were married, and under whose régime the Inquisition was started. I visited the cells and saw many of the dungeons of this building. In Madrid I visited the public square where the officials of the church and state assembled to celebrate the reading of the sentences of the Auto-da-fe to the victims before their being burnt at the stake. However, here in Barcelona is the only building that I found in Spain that bears the official seal of the Inquisition. In this building helpless men and women,

THE ANCIENT BUILDINGS OF THE INQUISITION IN BARCELONA. THE INSET IS A CLOSER VIEW OF THE INQUISITORIAL INSIGNIA DIRECTLY ABOVE THE DOORWAY.

whose only crime was that they did not believe exactly as the church wanted them to believe, were tortured with instruments invented by the perverted ingenuity of man to produce the most excruciating pain and torment. These tortures consisted of the breaking of the victim's bones upon the wheel and rack; the application of the thumbscrew and leg crusher; the branding of the flesh with red hot irons; the tearing of the body with pincers of steel; eyes were blinded; fingers cut off and tongues ripped out; some were submerged in water, others were beaten and racked beyond recognition.

All this was done to make them confess to the crime of heresy, that is, to the unbelief in the religion of those who were torturing them, that they might be taken to the public square and roasted to death.

During the period of the Inquisition, nearly three hundred years, it has been reliably estimated that more than one million victims were tortured and killed.

One of my purposes in traveling through Europe was to gather together as many as possible of the instruments of torture that were used during the Inquisition and establish in the United States a museum of these religious articles that may serve as an object lesson to man, that he should bear charitably and tolerantly with his fellow man upon the question of religion, and that such a hateful institution as the Inquisition shall never again exist upon this earth.

THE NEW SPAIN

MY trip through Spain convinced me that the people did not strike a moment too soon against the combination of church and king that was robbing them of their life's blood.

Spain offers the best example of the menace of a church-ruled country. Once the mistress of the world and a veritable paradise, it is now, after four hundred years of church rule, struggling for a place among the nations of the world.

Thomas Jefferson said that in every country and in every age the priests have been the enemies of liberty. Nowhere in my travels did I find this statement to be more pertinently true than in Spain. These parasites of the church have lived upon the labor of the people and have grown fat and sleek upon the fat of the land.

Only after visiting Spain can one understand the statement made by Alphonso, when in a conversation with Theodore Roosevelt, when the latter met him in London and offered him his sympathies in his conflict with the anarchists, the now exiled monarch replied: "It is not the anarchists that I am so much concerned about, it is the demands of the church that are a menace to my country."

SPAIN: A LAND BLIGHTED BY RELIGION

While traveling through Spain I saw enough mountains of granite to build a castle for every Spaniard and his family; enough uncultivated fields to supply fruits in abundance to all of its people. These fields have remained uncultivated because the land belonged to the priests and the church, and they were not concerned with its cultivation as long as an enslaved people supplied them with the best that the land produced.

In one stroke, in the most notable revolution of modern times, and with practically no bloodshed, the people of Spain completely separated themselves from the cancerous growth of the church.

The new Spain has all the potentiality of a new-born babe. The Future is hers.

The progress that has already been made by the new secular Republican government in rebuilding Spain and its efforts for the cultural advancement of all its people, is a remarkable achievement deserving the commendation of all liberty-loving and progressive peoples of the earth.

It is my fervent wish that the Spanish Republic thrive and prosper so its people may enjoy liberty and freedom, and contribute their share to the intellectual advancement of the world.

CPSIA information can be obtained
at www.ICGtesting.com
Printed in the USA
BVHW060042010720
582552BV00005B/860